For twenty-five years now and counting, Teen Ink has made it their mission to make sure the younger voices among us are heard in all their infinite energy and variety. In *Leave This Song Behind,* a rousing medley of hearts and minds range far and wide in coming to grips with the life of our times, happily reminding us why poetry remains one of the best of all possible ways for the up and coming to have their say. Compiled with eclectic zest and assembled under beguiling headings, this anthology keeps the juices flowing with infectious conviction. The editors have gone about their task with uncommon aplomb, and the avid teen bards have seized the day—making their presence felt in poems by turns buoyant, pensive, funny, funky, prickly, snappy, stirring, and all intensely alive.

—David Barber, Poetry Editor, *The Atlantic;* author of
two poetry collections, *Wonder Cabinet* and *The Spirit Level*

Using strong images to confront complicated issues, these poets are often perceptive beyond their years. Have no fear for the future of poetry, as long as young people like these continue to write, and places like Teen Ink continue to make their voices heard.

—Madeleine Fuchs Holzer, Educator-in-Residence,
Academy of American Poets

Leave This Song Behind is a robust, exceptional collection of diverse young people stretching, playing with, and recrafting the genre in a refreshing, compelling way. The contents of the anthology—arranged invitingly and using teen-friendly language—welcome multiple rereadings. Additionally, the remarkable quality of the poems is an important reminder that these poems can serve as apt mentor texts for teachers and other young poets in search of reading and savoring this body of mature, talented, quality literature. Most important, this anthology energizes young people to try their hand at writing poetry, too.

—Kimberly N. Parker, PhD, President,
New England Association of Teachers of English

W9-BSY-262

It's difficult to believe that teens wrote these astounding poems, but given the vibrant, youthful voices on display, who else could have written them? *Leave This Song Behind* is more than just a collection. It's a celebration.

—J. A. White, award-winning writer of *The Thickety* series

As young as these poets are, they know that the poem is an act of paying careful meditative attention to the smallest detail. These poems probe the most difficult situations with clarity, honesty, and wit. They reveal themselves to us through the images of the authors' lives, and they fill me with hope and optimism about a future of literacy and imagination.

—Sheryl Noethe, Montana State Poet Laureate Emeritus, Founding and Artistic Director of the Missoula Writing Collaborative

Teen Ink was very important and formative for me growing up. It wasn't just a place to see and read great art; Teen Ink helped me feel like I belonged.

—Ziggy Unzicker, winner of the 2013 Juneau Grand Poetry Slam; contributor, pages 88 and 122

Teen writers, if they are acknowledged, are often cited as being the voices of the future. But this anthology is not important because it "showcases the voices of tomorrow"—it is important because it contains the voices of today. Right now, teenagers have things to say about art, religion, sex, happiness, and so much more—and right now, if you care about these things, you'll listen.

—Anna Leader, winner of the National Poetry Prize for Youth in Luxembourg and the Stephen Spender Prize for Poetry in Translation; contributor, page 144

LEAVE
THIS
SONG
BEHIND

teen poetry at its best

A TEEN INK BOOK
Edited by Stephanie H. Meyer, John Meyer,
Adam Halwitz, and Cindy W. Spertner

Health Communications, Inc.
Deerfield Beach, Florida

www.hcibooks.com

Library of Congress Cataloging-in-Publication Data
is available through the Library of Congress

ISBN-13: 978-07573-1896-2 (Paperback)
ISBN-10: 07573-1896-7 (Paperback)
ISBN-13: 978-07573-1897-9 (ePub)
ISBN-10: 07573-1897-5 (ePub)

Publisher: Health Communications, Inc.
           3201 S.W. 15th Street
           Deerfield Beach, FL 33442–8190

Cover design by Sherri Hamilton
Cover art by Callie Fink
Interior design and formatting by Sherri Hamilton

We dedicate this book to our three amazing grandsons—
Orson, Tommy, and Matty—
as well as our longtime supporter, Barbara Field.

Stephanie and John Meyer

Contents

Let Me Tell You a Story   63

Shall I Compare Thee to . . . ?   83

Acknowledgments

First and foremost, we thank and acknowledge all the teenagers who have poured their hearts and minds into the pages of *Teen Ink* magazine and its ever-burgeoning website, TeenInk.com. This endeavor began as a way to help all teens feel they have a voice, and we're so grateful to the thousands of young writers who have furthered our mission by submitting their work. Their creativity has never disappointed us.

Since its creation, Teen Ink has depended on countless supporters, from our board, donors, and colleagues to our families and friends. This latest book was the product of many people, including our faithful volunteer, Barbara Field, who's been helping assess poetry for twenty years; our college intern, Natasza Gawlick, who aided this project greatly; and Sherri Hamilton, who designed the book's interiors and cover.

For this specific project, we must again focus on our constantly supportive publisher, HCI (Health Communications, Inc.). Our relationship with HCI spans more than fifteen fruitful years. We thank Peter Vegso, its captain; Ian Briggs, our editor; and, of course, all the support staff who have made this book possible.

Stephanie and John Meyer, Founders/Publishers of Teen Ink
Adam Halwitz, Book Development Editor
Cindy W. Spertner, Editor

Introduction

Instructions for living a life.
Pay attention.
Be astonished.
Tell about it.
—from "Sometimes" by Mary Oliver

Are there any better words for poets to live by? After all, isn't this how all poems are born? Poets look. They listen. They wonder and feel. And they are so moved—whether by astonishment, love, heartbreak, humor, or the desire to right injustice—that they need to write it down.

For over twenty-six years, teens from around the world have been sending their poems to Teen Ink, a place where words matter and teen voices are celebrated. Over the last decade alone, we have received and reviewed close to half a million poetry submissions. So when we decided to compile our first all-poetry anthology, we were blessed—and overwhelmed—with a wealth of choices. To prepare *Leave This Song Behind,* Teen Ink editors reread thousands of the poems we've featured in our magazine, and the final result is in your hands now: a collection of about a hundred of our favorites from the past five years.

What makes the pieces in this book so powerful that they stood out to us? After our initial "wow," we looked more deeply at each poem's strengths. We've divided *Leave This Song Behind* into seven sections based on the poetic techniques or qualities that moved us most. Vivid sensory details make some poems shine. Others catch our attention with simple, spare language. We chose other pieces because we were struck by their thoughtful use of form; compelling stories; strong figurative language; unexpected connections and wit; and fresh writing about familiar topics.

We hope you love these poems as much as we do. We are thrilled, as ever, to provide a place where young poets and the art of poetry can be celebrated. Teen Ink welcomes all teenagers' feedback and self-expression, and submitting to our website and print magazine is easy; just visit TeenInk.com. We look forward to being astonished by your work!

Foreword

As a young person growing up in the '60s, the first creative writing I ever did was poetry. Back in fifth grade, I hated most kinds of writing. So when our English teacher, Mrs. Auerbach, assigned each of us to compose a poem using rhyme and meter, metaphor, and, if we were really feeling ambitious, personification and alliteration, I can't say that I was thrilled.

Someone in our class raised a hand and asked what the poem was supposed to be about. (It wasn't me. The only time in school that my hand ever went higher than my shoulder was when we climbed ropes in gym.)

"Whatever you want it to be about," Mrs. Auerbach replied.

This response caused the members of our class to glance nervously at one another; we wondered if Mrs. Auerbach might have lost a few marbles. After all, this was back when children were expected to be seen and not heard, and the last thing students were required to have was an imagination.

"We can write about anything?" someone probably asked.

"Anything," replied our teacher.

This was seriously off the wall.

That night I went home and wrote a poem. And strangely, it wasn't painful. In fact, it was surprisingly painless. I wish I could remember what my poem was about, but I can't. All I know is that it was roughly the length (six stubby lines) of Carl Sandburg's "Fog," a poem we'd studied in class.

A few days later, when she handed our poems back, Mrs. Auerbach paused beside my desk to say that she'd liked my poem very much, and I might have even gotten a good grade if I'd taken the time to correct my spelling.

It was the first time in my life that anyone had ever complimented me on my writing. And from that moment forward I wrote day and night and—

Okay, that's not what happened. Actually, seven years would pass before I'd write anything creative again.

My own poetic output may have lapsed, but that didn't stop me from discovering and enjoying the writings of great poets. Also, the cultural revolution of the 1960s had begun and with it came the rise of singer-songwriters like Bob Dylan and Joni Mitchell. Suddenly poetry wasn't confined to books; it was everywhere—in our cars, homes, parks, street corners, cafés, and anywhere else that music was played or heard. Whether they realized it or not, people were surrounded by poetry on a daily basis.

I'm pleased to report that despite rumors to the contrary, the state of poetry today continues to be healthy and vibrant. To get a sense of what has changed in the past forty years, I spoke to Sam Sax, my son's friend who is currently on a James A. Michener Writing Fellowship (for poetry) at the University of Texas in Austin. Sam told me that he'd started out writing raps in high school. Then in college he discovered performance poetry.

"This work's gotta be shared in order to be relevant," he wrote recently. "It has to reach someone. The most important part of my journey as a writer has been surrounding myself with things that enrich my love of the art form, by reading like crazy, and putting myself in conversation with as many inspiring writers or poetry-crazy fools as I can."

Sam's advice to today's young poets: "Check to see if there's a local youth slam (they often come with really neat and caring mentors). Also, look into other kinds of writing groups. The Internet's an amazing resource to connect with other writers via YouTube or a proliferation of literary journals. Many writers offer online workshops you can pay to join."

It appears, based on Sam's report, that there are a lot more opportunities—to be published, to be heard, to be supported financially—for poets than when I was young. I'm gratified by this news. To me, poetry remains the singularly most beautiful form of word use.

Which brings me to this wonderful collection of poems, broken into sections that not only help categorize the work but reflect the very features we ascribe to, and would like to encourage as, good writing. What I especially love about this collection is the stories the poems tell, the worlds they introduce the reader to, the twists and unlikely connections we follow to the poems' conclusions. There can be no doubt about the creativity and talent of these young writers.

Let us celebrate what these young poets have done, for it is by no means easy. To stay on topic, evoke emotion, and use vivid imagery, to introduce an idea, flesh it out, and then resolve it with nuance

. . . this is the true work of writing, and it's why each one of these poems belongs in this collection.

As anyone who's gone online knows, there's a nearly infinite collection of very wise quotations about poetry floating out there in the cloud. But here's the one I'd like to end this foreword with. From the Mexican poet Octavio Paz: "To read a poem is to hear it with our eyes; to hear it is to see it with our ears."

Happy reading, and writing.

Todd Strasser

Author of *The Wave, Boot Camp, Fallout,*

and many other novels for teens

Come to Your Senses

Vivid imagery and strong sensory details

The primary pigment of poetry is the IMAGE.
—Ezra Pound

Clothesline

She liked to sit in the backyard
And watch the neighbor's laundry
Swing on the clothesline, crisp pale
Blue button-downs of the husband
Wrinkling in the half-wind, Summer
Sighing across the silky surface of
The twisting sundress, first one way,
Then the other, like soft hips
Swinging, one way, then the
Other, and when they were just
Washed and still wet they would
Flap and flick beads into the grass
That would flash fast down like
Little silver raindrops, one way,
Then the other.

Ariel Miller

Bluebells

the fat rope of tea
from the pot
to my mug
and the icicles all in a row
bulbs sit on the windowsill
waiting for spring
and I find an envelope
with pressed bluebells
from that day
you tucked them behind my ear
and ran your fingers through my hair
and when I got home
I pressed them in a dusty cookbook
letting them hold their fragile beauty longer
than the other sprigs it grew with
lucky them
I saved them
so I wouldn't forget
that you could be sweet
when you wanted
and even now they still haven't lost their scent

Indigo Erlenborn

She

sometimes she makes me want to tense the tendons on my neck and send my head smashing into my keyboard and maybe my skin and bones would, as they snapped and fractured, hit just the right keys and type a jumbled ode to beauty and wealth, forgotten forever when the circuits spark and smoke and the little copper nodes on the hard drive dig into my eyebrow and its brittle white plastic shell snaps and splinters

Charles C. Siler

More Summer

Oh summer is the
Damp fold of
My
Thin cotton skirt
Pressed
Between

Bleached bare
Legs

Salt powdered
Thick white
Flour
Over cherry-pie
Cheekbones

And the Wind's
Lank fingers
Dripping cold
Whitecap kisses
Down
My
Slick scalp
And along each
Hard
Peach-pit
Vertebra

Claire Weaver-Zeman

Year of the Dragon

The ginger on your plate smelled feebly of the rain last summer when
your parents visited weekly with smiles on their faces showing
    the kind of solidarity
even you dared to expect during this
roughest of times—
but they couldn't convince you of your
right to worth and you
never wandered back to that light down
by the river
where all the magic happened before you swallowed the bullet
    and slit your noose
and you fell out of love with life
in all honesty, everything died with your
first drops of blood kissing
linoleum, staining your heartstrings and straining the surface of
    water left
in everyone's chest after a meal with
that bitch—guilt
and while the ginger between the delicate rows of fish
    stank of the bygone
songs, the lyrics like rotting carcasses
with just enough light left
in the eyes to make you believe for even
a minute
that there is any sweet melancholy left,
the wasabi
cleansed the air with the odor of iodine
and the tea smelled like a gunshot

Miriam Himelstein

thoughts?

Year of the Dragon

I want "MGK"
branded on my calf
Kurt Cobain Etch A Sketched
across my stomach
a glowing uber-bright cool blue
Donor life butterfly
to commemorate my long-lost cousin
a hot pink heart on the nape of my neck
twisty vines arcing up my collarbone
"Stay Strong" prominent across the
silvered scars protruding from my
right arm
a ladybug skimming my thigh
your name on my foot
so every time I step on the ground
you're crushed into oblivion

Lauren Combs

And She Sang as the Chicken Crisped Up

When my grandmother made fried chicken it took on spiritual
 sublimity.
The way she would cradle the chicken with maternal caress.
And she would sing, not sing sing, but evolve into the mistress
 of song,
As the smell of paprika filled the dingy apartment.
And she sang with a wispy tone only cold nights can conjure.
And it was in this song, which soon became a chant as time and
 sound collapsed
and collided
That no longer was I listening but experiencing the sound of the
 woman's voice.
A voice that ripped trees from their thick roots and pulled the
 sun across the sky with chains of cloud.
And, of course, I stood there watching from across the kitchen
 and I felt the stiffness
of my bones,
Almost offending the situation, as if in my awkwardness I was
 taking away from the solar eclipse in front of me.
But she sang and I hated myself for standing with bones loud as
 engines when I moved them.
It soon became too much,
The shallow popping of chicken frying,
The woman before me exposing sound,
The creak of bone,
I felt as though the room around me was coming closer,
As if the world outside the poorly polished windows was
 beginning to cave in

And I felt nothing but the panic that I would be caught because
    of my loud bones.
Finally I screamed and this woman, in all
of her primal glory
Looked from her pan of browned chicken skin and stared
And I just stared,
Wishing my existence had not tainted the sanctified spectacle
    that occurred
some ten seconds ago.

Daniel Coelho

Fighting the Waves

I found my poem
splashing in four feet of icy water.
The strong smell of chlorine
stings my nose
and burns my dry throat.
I gag up all the cold water
I accidentally swallow
as my poem drifts farther out
into the giant wave pool.
I struggle to move forward
as the powerful waves push me back.
My poem travels all the way
to the deep end
shoving past rowdy kids
and serene adults.
My poem struggles to stay above
the tough waves
before it becomes completely
submerged in the arctic water.
I force myself to dunk my head
down below the cold liquid,
but I can't find my beloved poem.
It's lost.
That's when I know
it's time to get out.

Natalie Baddour

inverted biography

when you come out into this world
backwards,
breech baby, everything
holds its own weight.

at three, i held on tightly to a lamppost
breathed until the metal's taste burned my throat.
at seven, i fell deeply, irreparably in love
with the sound of a music box, with the sharp sting
of a paper cut.

i ran away from home
and swam in rivers for a year.
i let the foam lap against my thighs
curled my toes in the briny water
watched the fish choke writhing.
i came home and life was longer.

at ten, i stumbled into a book.
i smelled the pages' perfumed musk
i bounced atop the inky e's
waltzed with t's
fell asleep sprawled on a predicate.
at thirteen, i changed my name
once, twice, thirteen times
dina, agnes, tess, phoebe
when i stopped i couldn't remember who or how or why

i grew out my hair
so long it trailed fifteen miles behind me
one mile for every year—
so long i tripped and plunged down a rabbit hole

and
at seventeen, when i emerged,
head first this time,
i stepped on hard ground.

Julie Yue

I Would Like To

Savor pancakes,
syrup,
sip juice and ice as you
fix a disobedient strand of hair.

Rub my eyes over a crinkled newspaper
and ask you how you slept.
See in the skin around your eyes
how your bare feet shiver on the kitchen floor.

You draw a downy blue blanket around your shoulders.
I laugh as breakfast smells swim to my nose
Ready.

Bubble-spitting bacon, wrap the pieces in a paper towel
to keep them warm and oily.
Arms brush as you hand me dirty dishes.

Garrett Hinck

Dandelions

You notice the splinter in the curb at your feet,
where the earth has pushed through concrete and
a line of weeds has settled in a crevice.
The water-splashed, stained, laminated "Missing!"
poster for a black and white cat
is pinned to every available surface,
as if to better the chances of Fluffy remembering he has
    somewhere to be.
You notice the breeze stretching its fingers
through your hair and the light pit-
pat your worn-down Converse sneakers
make against the sidewalk, dandelions against
the base of a rusting chain link fence, facing upward toward a
sky expanding wider than the world could ever be.

Emma Foley

Less Is More

Simple language with a large impact

Poetry is language at its most distilled and most powerful.
—Rita Dove

I'll massage your tense shoulders

I've never wanted to be
thin white cotton
until today
when you lifted
your arms to stretch
and I couldn't
help but wonder
how wide
your wingspan would be
and how close
you could get to the sun
with those
shoulders of yours.

Chelsea McCoyle

Welcome Back, Darling

Welcome back from L.A.
Please do not attempt to unlock the door.
The locks have been changed,
I hooked the chain,
I even got a dog and he's waiting for you, salivating,
Because I haven't fed him in five days.
The shelter assured me he was vicious,
Hostile,
A danger to society
(You two might have been friends
In a past life).
Please do not attempt to contact me.
I am fine,
Safe,
Eating well
(No, I'm not at my mother's).
Go out, live your life.
I've FedEx-ed all of your belongings to
Your empty apartment on 75th.
And that shirt you spilled coffee on
Is waiting for you in the mailbox.
Please, dry clean and return it.
Thank you.
Please, don't have hard feelings.
I still find you attractive.

Miranda McClellan

Write What You Know

don't know calculus.
I don't know why the
quadratic formula is important.
I don't know what they put
in hot dogs or how
to make people like me,
and despite 150 hours
spent sitting in a classroom,
I still don't know anything
about chemistry.

But I do know how
to make coffee.
I know how to make
my best friend laugh.
I know how to properly
annotate a text (thanks
to my ninth-grade English teacher)
and I know what makes
rainbows appear.
I know why Simon Bolivar
said "Let's go as fast as
we can. No one loves us
here," before leaving for
exile in Europe, because I
know how it feels to live in
a place where no love exists.
I know that orchids are
the ugliest of flowers,

that's why I keep one in
my house at all times,
and I know why my grandmother
cried when I told her
I wanted to go into the arts.

I don't know if God exists,
but I know that morality does.
I don't know how to work
the cylindrical shell method
or solve for the integral
of a power series,
but I do know how to
keep my seven-year-old
cousin from crying.
And I'd take that
over calculus any day.

Mandy Seiner

my grandmother's kitchen

Never have I seen this place without
The old television propped
On the wooden table, the reception like
Cashmere and the sound deep
Underwater—and there is coffee
On the counter but it doesn't smell
Quite like coffee.

The curtains are fraying from
Moths, I assume, and there are droplets
Of dried red wine on the linoleum
Floor and I don't think that
She can see them anymore.
There are cups of pudding set out
For us and I think these forks
Are the understudies today.

I smile at myself from her
Refrigerator door, and my eyes are
Brighter than they are now, still
Sheltered from things that
One day they will see,
Such as my grandmother, shaking,
Fumbling with the back of her chair,
Saying, "Don't make me go."

Catherine Malcynsky

Heirloom

Last night at dinner,
Dad watched me push on
a bump on my back,
massaging it with three fingers
in circular motions.
Hold my neck up high,
make a straight line,
shoulders back,
the bump still there.

"Your mother had that, you know.
Just get used to it."

The only piece of you in me
is something I don't want.

Olivia Manno

Like Your Cat

You say
The Good only die young
Well then what about me?
I'm turning senile
Just like your favorite cat.
There he sits
Not caring about you
Not caring about himself
He grows very old
He starts taking longer naps
He starts to eat in privacy.
I'm just like an animal.
Put a collar on me when I grow old.
I'm not good
I'm not young
And I won't die.
But I do eat in privacy.
I live like your senile cat
And he's dying in your care.
For heaven's sake take care of me
Take good care of me.

Darius Kay

Souls Are Not Scientific

not an atom, she said,
not an atom doesn't love you
in my whole body.
and she kissed me but
I was too busy thinking about
how souls aren't
made of atoms
to notice

Anna Piper

Powder Blue with Roses

Do you
recall
the Easter Sunday
that I made my own dress?
Powder blue. I sewed on roses.
You said I looked nice
and I said,
"You too."
And you held me in
the pew when I cried
because the girl
behind us had a seizure.
Remember how we said
Amen
but we didn't really mean it.

Christina M. Gaudino

Charcoal Boat

when I was seven
I drew a boat in charcoal that I could so
nearly touch

and hear the waves that rocked under-
neath
that sang promises of the places it'd
take me

but when my fingertips touched
the paper
it smeared, and I realized that art
isn't magic

and ten years later I keep making the
same mistake
with people,

in thinking they are more than
they are

Callie Zimmerman

A Letter to the Past, Present, and Future Selves

1.
There will be days when your best friends are all in love
and you have been alone for three years.
These days will be hard, they will hurt,
they will sting with a blighting injustice
not felt since
Nathaniel Whatshisname broke all the crayons
in your 64-pack way back in kindergarten.
You will survive this.

2.
You are worth so much, I promise.
I firmly believe you will be okay.
You have so much love to give.
Don't spend it immediately on the
first stranger
who walks in and smiles at you.
The ensuing self-loathing
is not a form of medication.

3.
Being sad will happen often.
Having the opportunity to be involved in
the beautiful miracle of living happens
only once.
Do not give this up for anything.
Do not set yourself on fire.

Do not crash your car into the telephone pole.
Do not drink your body weight in tequila.

4.
It's okay to drink yourself to sleep
with NyQuil
every once in a while.
I know it's easier than lying for hours alone
in your massively empty bed
thinking of everything you'll never have.
Do not make this false sleep a habit.
This summer may not be yours, but your
life is.

5.
You are not obligated to tell anyone
anything.
I cannot stress enough
how important you are.
You must find something that makes
all the voiceless screaming in your head
a little more bearable
and you must clutch it in your bones
with every ounce of strength you have.

Sofia Wesley

a preposterous poetical proverb for practical people

when someone asks you
   do you like my outfit

it is wise to say yes

to anyone not in your

immediate family

and even then

be cautious

Meredith Thomas

Not Enough

I am lonely and loved
My mother's arms hold me close
beneath warm sheets on wintry days
and believe me, I wish
that this was enough

Rachel Hsu

After All This Time

After all this time, I still have
posters on the walls
dreams on the ceiling
nowadays I forget to check
and see if the moon is waning
Sometimes I just want
to go outside and
sit on the porch
and watch the cars go by

Christal E. Walker

Get into Shape

Poems that play with structure, form, and sound

In Poetry, a new cadence means a new idea.
—Amy Lowell

orange hospital bracelet

i see you blurry burgundy
when you talk about heart problems
though your shirt is gray.
the hospital is terrifying,
white sterilized to
death.

i learned from waiting
room magazines that blood is
blue until it's oxygenated, and
osteosarcoma is highly curable
unless it takes a liking to
you.

dr. green talked to you without
me, like preparation,
and i prayed to your red iv drip—
please don't leave me
here, pale alone and
alive.

Sophia Shelton

serena

orange hopeful bracelet

my sister was born as a holy mess, like
an appendix like a grenade, a heart like a
printer jamming when your final paper is
due in five minutes, veins like chewed
straws, salt columns for legs dissolving in
water. like, she's the blessed saint of falling apart.
like, picture this brown angel woman on
her knees. like, serena dies. like, serena lives.

like, picture this: chaos made of water and
words. serena's brown body is a pitfall
of a body, her mouth is a sinkhole of a
mouth, and i can see ships capsizing between
her teeth. like, seismic-shiver mouth. like,
she rots quickly to cold soil and flies. like,
her body doesn't even matter. like, her
body is all that matters.

like, she is made of body and of nothing
but body.

like, she's not ashamed as she realizes she is
our father's daughter. like, does it even
matter. his sisters died when they were
twenty-three and twenty-five, and
serena and i know we are going the same
way. like, even when i feel like dust in
the bottom of a sarcophagus, i remember
that this is a tomb, that there must be a body.

our aunts were not immune, and they
died for it. sea-bound ladies, salt-
cracked stomachs, dried oasis eyes
and i did not want to be born into a
cornucopia of dead women, but i was.
like, we both were. i can feel the girls
cutting crop circles within us,
telling us things we can't understand yet,

like, don't go outside without your
shoes on, like, you will meet a girl
who came from where you came from but
you won't know it until it's too late,
like, your grandmother keeps our rooms
like they were when we died, like,
we need to teach you to love the things
you have to let go of. like, body is only body.

Alana Solin

O, Father Time

That Father Time
No dad of mine
He came to see
The work I'd done
With riddled rhyme
And rigid thoughts
In a fragrant, smooooooth
Pleasant lyric.

But

I said to time,
"You have no place
To hold me to
Your pointless race
On abstract tracks
Devoid of space
No depth but what
I give it."

And

I think I'll watch
My own damn clock,
Those loving hands
And the smiling face
You're just a watch
You heartless thing
No dad of mine,
O, Father Time.

Jessica Covil

chinese politics (over dim sum)

tea me,
king me—this is, after all
a game of checkers we are playing here.
simple, yet understated,
with more thoughts than could ever
be spoken in one move.
i lift up my tea cup and watch the
muddy liquid spill over,
burning my hand.

pawn me,
play me.
pawn me off as your
lacking in some aspects and definitely
understated but she has potential daughter
because we all know that bragging
isn't good for the soul—
praise will only
make the Gods take me away.
(i tap my plate twice with my chopsticks,
they can probably hear my obvious
disbelief)

dim me,
sum me
up as nothing more than
a banana (yellow on the Outside
white on the Inside)
peel me open and bite down

on cold flesh, frozen for
two weeks because you had great plans
for a chocolate-covered banana, but
forgot about it.

i am me—
i am a me waiting for
the conversation to commence in
slow one-upping "have you heard that my daughter got into Yale"
(suck on that)

"Harvard"

(Yale is second place for losers)

"MIT."

(my son will be the next Bill Gates)
"Lily is taking four hours of ballet per
day and
she still manages to finish her homework"
(she is so dedicated) "what about your daughter? what does
    she do?"

(can you beat that?) would you like another dumpling?
"my daughter is working very hard; she won prizes in writing"
(she does nothing. i am watching my figure.)

chinese politics is never good for my
self-esteem.
i pick at the meat on my plate,
half listening, half understanding,
half ashamed.
half is less than a whole.

Eda Tse

Genevieve Carnell

It was silly, this editing. The stories would never see the light of day. But we passed passages and chapters and thoughts. Brainstorms the size of hurricanes. She would get upset when I removed all the extra letters. American, I would remind her. She would sigh and add back the "u's" when I wasn't looking.

Moria Crowley

The Sistine Closet

Dear Michelangelo,
I've heard the rumors they whisper about you,
And I can't help but wonder
If you've heard about me too.
There is a church in my town
Where they aren't allowed to say my name anymore,
Where the pastor says "we don't talk about her here."
I wonder if anyone has ever damned us both
In the same breath

Dear Michelangelo,
They say you painted men
More longingly than you painted women.
They say you freed David from his prison
In the hopes that he would free you from yours.
They say your hands were clasped in his
When they should have been clasped in prayer.
They say there was a man in your heart
And his name was not God

Dear Michelangelo,
I have been painting girls with my tongue.
I have rolled them around in my mouth
And when I spit them out on the paper
They always arrange themselves into poems,
But I can never get the endings right.
People keep telling me they're supposed to be happy

Dear Michelangelo,
We both know that love
Is hardly ever a happy ending.
We know that some hands can never touch,
That they are separated by too many locked doors
And not enough keys.
We know that some people are games of hide and seek
Where no one is doing any seeking.
We both know how it feels to hide

Dear Michelangelo,
When they ordered you to paint the Sistine Chapel
Did you laugh at the irony?
Did you consider painting it differently?
Did you think about painting the hands touching?
Did you want to paint Adam
Wrapped in the loving embrace of another man?
Did you want to put a speech bubble above God's head
That said "It is okay to love him"?

Dear Michelangelo,
Why aren't the hands touching?
Why aren't the fingers interlocked?
Why isn't one sweaty palm clinging to the other?
Even in our wildest fantasies,
Even in our most famous masterpieces,
The fingertips will always be a few inches apart,
The people will never be happy.
What does that say about us?

Dear Michelangelo,
When I finally escape from here
I want to visit your Sistine Chapel.
I am slowly realizing that not all closets are small and dark.
Some closets are sixty-eight feet tall
And covered in angels,
But they are still closets.
They are still prison cells packed full of skeletons
And the baggage you are too embarrassed
To leave lying around when you have company over

Dear Michelangelo,
When I can't sleep at night I wonder where you are now.
I wonder if heaven exists.
I wonder if God was waiting for you at the gates,
If he looked at you and said
"Don't listen to them. Of course you can come in.
Of course you can come out now."
Michelangelo, tell me there are no closets in heaven.
Tell me I will be allowed to walk down the street
Holding her hand.
Michelangelo, paint me every shade of beautiful you know.
Make me the rainbow that is missing from your ceiling.
Michelangelo, promise me they'll let us in.

Hannah Livernois

To a friend, in answer to his existential crisis

You ask me, I imagine,
over a strong cup
of Turkish coffee
in that way that is both abrupt
for the sake of it
and shocking for the sake of it
and vague in that way that makes me
grit my teeth like there's a toothpick in the middle and I just can't,
no I can't

let

go.
So you shock
just to put shock to your name and
fold in a hundred thousand
potential answers and
you're not looking at my face but
looking for me to say
that I hate, too,
the sugar packet
in my hand and
I'm thinking that maybe you hate me
for not taking

my coffee

black.
And meanwhile you've

smoked through your last
hand-rolled cigarette.
So when you ask me,
in that way you have, through

thin eyes and

tight lips and

ears closed
against me through a fog of semi-organic carcinogens,
I know
and you know
and the whole goddamn world knows
how wonderful that
unwashed
and unseen
and untold
corner of your mind is
that asks such kaleidoscopic questions.

Ilana Feldman

Another Poem About You and the Sink in Your Downstairs Bathroom

"What's wrong?" He said.

Well for starters it confuses me why my pen runs out of ink in
    the middle of the sentence as if I had never been writing at all
    as if my pen was trying to tell me to shut up
I don't understand why my mom doesn't
listen to a single word at mass
all she does is lick her fingers and flip through the book of hymns
like she's some kind of important thing that already knows what
    God wants us to think every single week
and the sink in your downstairs bathroom drains really slowly
    sometimes I stand there and stare
I pretend I'm watching my life circle around the drain slowly
    until it gets sucked away
for the rest of forever and you know
sometimes it bothers me that I'll never see any of the water
    droplets ever again
I think it's weird that my dad calls my mom's parents mom
    and dad
he should just not call them anything
because they aren't his parents he is just guilty by association
like that detention I got in eighth grade
I would like very much if my best friend didn't want to kill herself
    because I think it would
make my shoulders feel less like they are caving into my shoulder
    blades
I am horrifically annoyed that no
one and no-

thing is in love with me because my walls
are painted red and it makes me feel like I should feel passionate
    about something
or someone or anything just anything at all but in all honesty
I am really tired
I hate that I can't stop thinking about you because I read an
    article that said
you could make yourself believe anything you want so I told
    myself 537 times
I counted
that I didn't care a bit about you, no offense
and I think my
ankle is
sprained.

Angela Sabo

Dear Me, From Me

Dear Sam,
Sooooo
This is awkward
I'm sorry
we haven't spoken in a while.
The thing is
I've been really awful lately
you deserve better than me
and I want to apologize

You were a gold bust that I painted silver
A stock car that I forced to only make
right turns
I was your glitchy GPS
In 35 feet ask out Jessica in front
of all of her friends
recalculating
in one week use three y's when you text "heyyy" to Mandy
recalculating
in 22 hours wear crocs
recalculating
in 3 seconds fart
recalculating
From now on just give up

I had good intentions
you are the best me I ever could
have asked for

So I'm sorry
I hope that you can forgive me

Sincerely,
Sam

Dear Sam,
Don't get me wrong
It is nice to hear from you again
and
for once
you're right
this is awkward.
because actually things have been
really great without you

You convinced me
that every success came with fine print
which said (in size 4 font)
"Ummm. actually you still suck"
that every stride forward was three yards
too short
that any time I did something well
there were 50 other people there who
did it better
and I believed you
You stuck a funhouse mirror in
my bathroom
that made me too big in some places
and too small in others

You held a magnifying glass up to my
imperfections and put them on instagram
#poppingpimples
You super-glued velcro to my lips
when I tried to speak
and you shoved a towel down my throat
when I wanted to sing
You stuffed my personality in a locker
wrapped my arms in a straitjacket
and tied refrigerators to my ankles
You sculpted my shadow in someone
else's image
and made me follow it

You'd yell
Sam, Shut up
Sam, walk faster
Sam, walk slower
Sam, be cool

Sam, smile
Sam, be quiet
Sam, Shut up
Shut up
shut up
Sam
Sam!
Sam!!

I love who I am
I wake up thankful that I am me
I love every
wrinkle
pimple
scar
failure
success
memory
fist
hug
smile
that makes up who I am
You may have stuffed a towel down
my throat
but I
chewed it
swallowed it
and now there's a fire in my belly
You may veto my satisfaction
but I've got a two-thirds majority in
my gut that says
you can suck it
I am going to send you a postcard that reads
GREETINGS FROM I DID IT
with no return address

Sincerely,
Sam

Sam Little

blue base

water weighs nothing.
it is
liquid glass between my
outstretched hands
as I drift to the bottom

and settle like sand.
don't tell me to come back up

for I can only speak in
bubble curtains
thick and sparkling clear.
instead join me

here at the bottom

of the busy world
where the blue is deep and soft
and silent.

Kristian Rivera

With Every Atom of My Being

the blood red
curtains seem to be
draped across the sky.
isn't it beautiful?

she whispered to the
blond-haired girl
sitting next to her.
yes, answered the girl.

she stood next to me in the lake one day.
we're so tall in the water. our legs: never-ending

crooked lines. i watched her fingers draw out
ripples that grew and grew, then strained and buckled.

a dim light illuminated the wrinkles in her father's eyelids.
she was wearing the yellow dress he bought her.

she is the color of the earth
(the kind that would get on your shirt when you dug for worms)

with nighttime eyes. she's not all there in the head.
neither am i. well, i'm all there in my fingers, and
my father says i'm all there in my heart, and that's
what matters, because without our heart our blood can't flow.
that was what she told me when i brought the matter up to her.

her father was full of fire, but very kind. and sometimes she hid
    from him,
and sometimes she talked about the stars and birds with him. he
    was very fascinated.

especially by the sky. i once told her i thought she was too pretty
    to be lonely.
she told me she wasn't lonely and had all the people she needed. i
    guess it was me who

was lonely. i watched her dance at the edge of a cliff. windswept
    with her hair the color of dirt.
the roar of the wind always filtered out my voice from the air. she
    looked upon

my countenance once. you would have thought i was a quiet
    admirer from the look on her
face. all five senses are filled with salty waves and sand, and i'm
    running, and i forget in which direction,
but i'm running because i knew she was
too close and the rock was pushed over.

Michal Zweig

It's My Job

Masochism is
my forte, I think I'll make
a career of it.

Then my parents will
be proud of me for using
my talent toward the

Future of my well-being

Katie Grey Lewellen

The Second Coming

I thought I saw Jesus shirtless and
sweaty today,
and I thought, what of the bodily functions of the divine?
That sort of thing really stinks of decay.

He ran right into the street, into a car;
I saw him ricochet,
but he stood up, raised a hand. "I'm okay, I'm fine."
I thought I saw Jesus shirtless and
sweaty today.

It probably wasn't Jesus, but I've gotta say
I thought I felt a psalm burning down
my spine.
That sort of thing really stinks of decay.

People gaped at him from windows of
their cafés;
maybe they thought their espressos would turn to wine.
I thought I saw Jesus shirtless and
sweaty today.

You can walk on water, but concrete
gives way.
Son, this isn't the higher place. This is the High Line.
I thought I saw Jesus shirtless and
sweaty today.
That sort of thing really stinks of decay.

Alana Solin

Sincerely, Perspective

Dear (fractured sense of) self,
you aren't just a pair of milky wrists
heavy with the footprints of
crazed explorers.

You aren't just the rhymes
that translate like
soft molasses and
melt on your tongue.

You aren't just the number of
milligrams or
"I won't miss you's"
or dry Sundays.

You aren't the thinning liquor
you're swallowing back
between broken sobs and
perhaps truths.

Dear (the rawest form of my) self,
you are
real.
You are
glowing.
You aren't
just runny punctuation.
You are the story.

Samantha Park

Let Me Tell You a Story

Narratives, true and fantastic

Stories are the creative conversion of life itself into a more powerful, clearer, more meaningful experience.
—Robert McKee

Anonymous, Framed

The girl is at the dock. You see her
like a photograph, following all this
rule-of-thirds nonsense; she at the dock,
which is dark and decaying and natural
against the sandpapered ocean, and maybe
a seagull, blurred, cast upon a wooden seat. She
has brown hair, graced past her shoulders, scattered
like shells on the thin sandbar,
slightly lifted in the breeze off the sea.
Her dress is too—floating like a buoy,
white and matching the seagull's pent
dedication to the waves. You expect her
to turn; you expect her to dip a toe
into the water that will send shivers
along her spine; you expect so many things
from the girl you don't know, sitting at the dock
watching noon clock by: lazy, rolling.
She is slipping toward the edge, slipping
to the moment where gravity simply overcomes,
where she is the anchor, you are the soft sound
of a wave falling along the beach, a shell cupped
against the ear, the silver sun's glare.
You are across the dock; you are outside
the picture frame. She is within, shining.

Kunal A. Sangani

bread for my soul

The afternoon I walked out of your life,

I made a stop by a tired bakery, my hands dug in my pockets. I
needed a moment

to feed; I'd run out of your soul to digest, and I was wasting away.

Behind the counter, there was a woman with her dog, a tiny
woman,

a large dog, but for reasons I was too foolish to see, she towered
over the

canine, her white hair strung out like a lioness.

"Child, you look tired" she said. I counted out the change for

a filled loaf of bread; I didn't want to talk with her, she looked
dangerously

at peace with her life, the dog content to guard his mistress's
desires and fight for her will

while there was myself, running and hiding from the damage I
caused in my past footsteps.

But her voice was too overwhelming and I stopped reaching for
my pennies. Dog came and sat by

my foot, she came and wrapped those withered arms around my
glassy shoulder-bones while my eyes bled my emotions.

The pastry began to crumble between my fingers, and the red
center began to leak from between each

grainy impression of wheat. I had cried before that day, but I
cried the hardest

when she whispered that you had really been a leech into my ear.
Hours came and

went, I'd breathed a few times, before giving my farewells and
walking away.

(That bread become my body)

aiden gamble

Smelling Crayolas

Crayola, smell. Starbucks grande
soy chai tea latte
drops. He laughs with pride
like Rosie Ruiz. Spills.
Sienna, indigo. Violet.
I sit in the "Kara Stinson:
Mayor of Shits-ville 2010!" bathroom stall.
Cherry tomatoes
impaled by my spork.
Sunset orange. Sky blue, teal.
Broken under
the pressure of sweaty palms and coloring
books. Forgotten.
Dried mango in a
ziplock bag. Snack size. Enough
to make it. Someone
purges in leftward toilet. Leaves.
Heels click on
counterfeit marble flooring.

I heard her beautiful fucking
laugh down the hall from my English
class during first period. Then we'd see
each other in the hall
and she stumbles over my name
but she was so damn nice
that it didn't matter. She was trying to
be kind.

And was I Sofia or Sofie anyway? I didn't even know.
And then we'd part and go to homeroom.
And after, during second period. Theatre.
I'd see her again.
she'd tell everyone to call her daddy
and she'd say things like white boys all day and the wall grabbed
   my weave.
Then she'd somersault.
Like who the hell does that? But we loved it.
She lived to make people laugh. She'd see me
alone. And she'd come over. Are you okay?
I'd nod my head and smile, polite. Somehow she'd see through
me. But she also could see that I needed my space.
She wouldn't push me. With her,
knuckle sandwich for lunch graduated
to knuckle McChicken and a lack of
understanding
would be met with an incredibly secure
Wh-what?! On the last day
she said bye to me.
And just like that she was gone.
Never to smell Crayola crayons
Or a high school bathroom
again.

Sofia Engelman

First Law of Motion

today
in Physics
with the teacher who
says friction is everywhere, says
graphs are
beautiful,
and the dim lights
and their heads on their desks
dreaming of satellites,
not love,
never love,
he steals
Newton's equations,
blue ink
from another universe,
to keep.

it's been three months
since the kiss,
last summer
camp,
slimy, stumbling,
dark,
confused tongues,
crickets,
i think i am standing still,
inertia.

it scares me, sometimes,
i forget if your hair
feels like feathers
or not,
i forget if it's earl grey
or english breakfast
you drank
at night.
but
objects in motion
remain in
motion.
and time moves,
and,
maybe,
i move.

Isabel DeBré

to sophia

the highways of Boston
must be bordered by dead men.
I saw one lying there once,
blanketed by streetlights in late July,
watched it come up beside my car
like a pale stationary fish,
thought for one crazy minute
that he was sunbathing
on the side of the road
in the middle of the night.

looking for an address I'd
only seen on Christmas packages,
watching the neon numbers
slide away into the dark,
I felt like
I'd been driving for hours
and we didn't have the time to slow down
or dwell on it
or wonder why he hadn't been
wearing any clothes.

I found your door at last,
was welcomed by sweat stains
and vaguely remembered faces
and you in the middle of it all,
"Sorry, we don't have any
air conditioning," but

I told you it was all right
and followed you upstairs,
dizzy, tired, overwhelmed,
glowing with heat and the joy of reunion.

we sat out under the bug zapper
on your tiny side porch,
getting used to each other's voices
all over again.
I remember watching the mole on your upper lip
the same way I did
the first time we met,
startled by how little you had changed,
wondering if you thought
I had changed too much.

sometimes when I dream,
the dead man still appears
tangled up with salsa and lawn sprinklers,
swimming in your bathtub
beside our grass-stained feet.
sometimes when I come home and
check my e-mail,
when I have no new messages,
I wonder if I ever saw him
(or you) at all.

Emma Burn

Reading at the Lake

I went to read a book by the lake at 2:18 this afternoon,
because I'd lied about needing to be somewhere at 2:30,
and I needed a place to go. So I went.

I bent the front cover back, so no passersby could see
the uncircumcised man on the front,
because it was Yehuda Amichai, who knows lapsed Jewry
better than anyone but me and
all the other children of the Diaspora.

I was clumsy with the cover, because the wind was cold,
and my fingers were cold,
and the deserts from the pages did their jobs too well.

The other walkers would sometimes glance at me
lying on my front on the bench, my left leg crooked so
the spots where the cartilage is strange
don't throb and whine.
I looked back at them, sometimes,
from behind my backlit fringe, because I wanted to see
what they thought of a young girl reading a book
with a bent-back cover and her feet in the air,
and not have them see me.
Everything's a performance.

I won't remember the people I looked at tomorrow,
when my fingers have thawed out,
and I wonder if I should have attended services yesterday,
and the patch of mud behind my knee has rubbed off,
but maybe one of the people who looked at me will remember
a young girl, hiding the front of her book with her hand,
looking at them through a veil of hair.
And hey, I have this poem.

Beatrice Waterhouse

Prometheus

The summer I was eight years old,
my sister found a pack of sparklers
hidden in the garden shed
slim sticks, black and cobwebbed,
that had lain dormant, forgotten
behind a rusted red tricycle.

We coveted fire,
smuggled the sparklers
behind my pillow,
until the night was ready
to be set aflame.
It was midnight,
the dark heavy with July air,
and we were alone
two skinny little girls,
twisting secretly through the darkness
with a pack of sparklers
clutched firmly
between two sweating hands.

My sister was never afraid
of fire
but as she lit the first match
I drew away, eyes wide and searching
for burns, for shadows,
for something living,
some knowing spirit

studying us and
our faraway secrets.
She was alive
with excitement, lips painted red
with the remains of melted cherry popsicles,
flushed and giggling at the power
she held in that single shining sparkler.
It was her eyes that convinced me,
in the light of stolen fire,
to reach out, strike match after match
and watch our secrets burn.

That night, we set fire
to every charred sparkler.
Sweat dripping,
barely breathing,
we held the sparklers
against the dark sky
writing in flame
the things we could never say
before dusk; carving the letters
in fire and smoke and leaving them
to smear the perfect faces
of the stars,
if only for a moment.

The sparklers died and died,
and we lit them one after the other
with impatient desperation.
When finally there was only one sparkler,

only one more chance to speak
in flames,
we stared at each other,
studying scabby knees
and scars
and pink-cheeked delight.
We took the sparkler
between our two dusty hands
fire dancing
in our eyes,
as we struck a match and cradled
the flame,
breathing life
into our single shining sin.

Eden Hartley

Clementines

Every day,
under a school desk,
I carefully kindle a fire in my hands.
Piece by piece
I rip the textured skin off,
And the tart juice bathes my fingertips.
The continents of Clementine peel
Are lightly piled in the top right corner
Of the surface.
I savor the sweet ocean
On the tingling taste buds of my
Tongue.

Tomorrow
I will forget to bring a Clementine.
And Mr. Drallos will explain the relationship
Between modern
Sociopolitical standpoints
And the representative democracy
Of ancient Rome.
But the only thing I can focus on
Is the aroma of Clementines.
My imagination will ignore the reality
My mind will reach far and stretch wide
To the citrus scent in my dreams.
Across the aisle of seats,
I observe your soft hands
Under a school desk,
Carefully kindling a fire.

Ayah Alghanem

Walk-out

the lead actor could not
sing. I was not the lead
and I didn't pretend I could sing.
the piece was in four and thirteen
bars in, I felt like latching on to
your neck like a leech and whispering
for us to get out of the opera hall.
what disturbed me was the dissonance
which reminded me too much of
us. we had graphite-colored conversations
almost like they were
salads of undressed greens.

we left. an echo of an F# escaped into
the corridor when you held the door for me. still
with the tune in my head, I drank some water,
bowing my head to
lean into the fountain. paint
chips looked like misplaced music notes.
as the curtain fell, ending the second
act, you put your arm around my waist,
offering passionately but redundantly to
take me away. yes, I said,
I'll leave this song behind.

Isabel Gwara

She walks with her head held high,
a grin on her face.
A denture-less smile.
It scares me a little
but she looks nicer without them.

You know she's in a good mood
when she plops herself at the piano and starts to sing.
Now, don't get me wrong: she has the voice of an angel.
But when either my sister or I act up,
My mom decides who sits next to Grams in church
    for our punishment.
She sings loud enough for God to hear.

Tia Roberson

Grams and Tonic

Light-up shoes were so '90s.
But my grandmother doesn't think so.
She apparently still thinks they're in style.
I felt like I accomplished something in life when I passed her
    by in height.
I was eight.

I swear, the woman is always in her own world.
Humming, laughing, and singing to herself.
I wonder how old she thinks she is—
Six? eighteen? twenty-one?
You couldn't guess by the way she dresses.
One day it's overalls
and the next she's wearing a belly-peeking halter.
Personally, I prefer the fleece penguin pajamas.

I remember she used to have three goats.
Gin, Tonic, and Brandy—
also her favorite drinks.
You can always count on my grams to pull out
the step stool
and make her way to the top shelf
to grab her Southern Comfort.
I suppose she feels classy drinking it out of a wine glass.

impatient

we tried
to take the shorter way
back home, but instead
we bumped into the
night train, carrying
cargo and slinking heavily
past our rain-covered
car windows
for fifteen minutes

minutes before, i held
the picture of the
idyllic college campus
between my thumb
and forefinger

watched the guidelines
turn into snakes, writhing
beneath my skin

and wondered if i'd ever

get anywhere, and this

this is how i realized
that shortcuts
don't make anything
easier

Kalina Zhong

Shall I Compare Thee to . . . ?

Powerful similes and metaphors

*A poet is, before anything else, a person
who is passionately in love with language.*
—W. H. Auden

Pomegranate

It's a delicate surgery, slicing open
the grenade.

With the urge to rip off
the tough sunburn and head straight
to the center, peeling back
purse lips to reveal the
jackpot,
I cut.

I've broken its crown—worse than a heart.
Clusters crackle, ruby mine, all mine.

I'm the monster. It's my job to devour.
Forgetting the milky membrane, I kiss,
I sputter rose juice, I stain everything.
Rows of tangy
seeds gleam and cry.

Luscious universes unfold. I'm always
opening new parts, discovering. I am a blood
sucker, a sap licker,
a star eater.

Claudia Taylor

Jazz Girl

She, I have decided, is like jazz.
Not big band, not Glenn Miller's brassy swing
or blasting trumpets.
Cool jazz, smoky quiet New Orleans jazz,
born from boredom and a need for variety.

Her face is a "Gloomy Saturday,"
Her hands "My Funny Valentine,"
Her legs "God Bless the Child"
(Who's got his own, who's got his own,
and doesn't that sound perfect for my ever-independent girl?)

Her smile comes quick like Ella and Cole Porter,
Fast and complicated lyrics to "You're the Top,"
even as she murmurs hello;
her tears come soft and slow like Ms. Kitt wishing
to be Evil.

She moves with the grace of Norah Jones' voice,
breathes like "Feeling Good,"
and sleeps like "Sinnerman" live,
all fits and starts and silky-calm smug uncertainty.

I wonder what it would be like
to hum these notes into her shoulder,
see if, even in her sleep,
she can feel the vibration, free of
conscious embarrassment.

I want to listen to the deep drumbeat
of her dedicated heart,
tap the accompanying snares
on the taut, tender skin of her thigh.
Hear the melody of brightly rushing blood
in the arches of ticklish feet,
the descant of comfortable breath,
of gentle wheezes in familiar lungs.

I want to memorize all of her varied
and impossible rhythms, play them back
in high fidelity and surround sound, and then,
when I have been filled with
the sound and taste and brightly colored life of
her, I want to dance.

And maybe, someday,
I will find a way to keep her just like jazz,
endless and influential and a constant companion
for all these many, endless days.

Beatrice Waterhouse

Don't Fall in Love

Don't fall in love with a girl who reads
she'll overanalyze every word
and she'll never understand why
people aren't paperbacks
and she'll write in your corners
search for a plot in your veins
and make a metaphor of your broken heart

don't fall in love with a girl who reads
she'll make notes in your margins
and skip to the good parts
she'll bend your spine back
just a little too far
and when she's sleepy
she'll skim pages
always forgetting her place

don't fall in love with a girl who reads
because she'll fall in love with
last chapters and final words
and the ending will always be
her favorite part

Claire Podges

My Hands Are Empty

Your green, green dress made me laugh.
This is as nice as it will ever get,
You said, and your knees were bruised
Above red shoes ill-matched and still wet
With puddles of dirty rain.
Would you like to dance? My hands
are empty,
And your dress is green as love and coarse as memory

We are made of layers, layers, layers,
That has always been the way
And in season we shed these layers
Until there is nothing left to lose

And when you went home and peeled off that green, green dress,
Inside there was a girl
Small and fair and young as anything;
Inside her was a woman
Strong and lovely, coursing energy,
And inside her, an old, old soul
An old, old heart,
A tree
Green as love and coarse as memory,
Slowly
Shedding
Its leaves

Still, I cannot abstract you,
But what will be left of us
When we have lost every layer
And shed every shell?
What will we find together
In the cupped hollow of the hands of
friendship's love?
Who can tell?

Love is
God is
Love
In empty hands

Waltz (2, 3)

Waltz (2, 3)

We danced the most terrible waltz (2, 3)
Oh, but our words danced incredibly free
And so sparse like the dances of stars
That our feet no longer mattered to us;
We were alone and time was ours
(2, 3)
(2, 3)
2,
3,
Fin

Thank you
This is as nice as
It will ever get,
You said.
Funny, I was thinking the same thing

Ziggy Unzicker

food and wine

you're burnt onto the bottom of everything
I know,
like a bone, or a bad
joke, I choke you out
whole, of course and
wipe the blood from my mouth
pick you out of my teeth and stare
emotionless at the black mess
at the bottom of the pan, take a drink
from the bottle in my hand only to discover
your spirits burning
the back of my throat, fermented
years ago and just now opened
and it's too late
you've already intoxicated me
again, I can feel the world
slowly falling away;
fork falls to table
glass falls to floor
in a crash splatter tinkle carpet stain
and the rest of you spreads
and takes root
impossible to remove
as my poisoned frame lands
on the rug we bought together
last spring.

Morgan Chesley

knees on neon (a hymn)

i'm tired
as mirages scratch up roof shingles
like dandruff flakes.

sleepy sleepy feet
cross over sidewalk stars,
the mountain-sky-touch the corners
kind of sidewalk stars

and maybe, maybe
that's what stars look like in space
when their light has been unplugged,
the terse OPEN at the bar window as you enter,
the cat-eyed blur of it
as you leave.

Andrea Wade

Furrow

knees on neon (a hymn)

Bruises she left on the insides of my thighs:
Like postage stamps, like Girl Scout badges, like wax seals on
    envelopes, like stickers on Granny Smith apples
She told me,
In the dark, on a blanket spread on the floor,
That she had waited three years to tell anyone that she was sick
That she was dying
And that
If she had told someone sooner
They would have been able to do something.
It's not your fault. Don't ever, ever think it's your fault.

I can see your spine through the skin of your back:
Like cat-eye marbles rolling on the blacktop, like pistachios in a
    plastic bag, like dice clicking across the Monopoly board
She told me
In her room, at dusk, with her arms tight around my waist
That sometimes she would be so tired that she would hear things
Sounds, voices,
Buzzing in a chaotic fog
In her hospital room, at night
And I remembered when
I heard the same noises in my head.

Furrows in flesh:
Like the sidewalk stuttering against a crack, like chalk scraping
    on concrete, like heat shimmering restlessly over the highway

She told me
Through the heavy afternoon, without our shirts on
That she hated the rough seams on her
stomach
And looked for marks on my body:
My cheek, my shin, the crook of my elbow.
I could only say
That I loved the scars, because they are a part of her
And spell stories more powerful than any poetry I've read.

You wouldn't have wanted to know me when I was in the
    hospital:
Like a man who has never blinked, like a moth with cuts on its
    wings, like a skeleton made of stacks of buttons
She told me
On her bed with the window open, the
dogwood trees shedding white petals
That she thought she was going to die when she was
    nine years old
Some days
She wishes she had
And I told her that I knew what it felt like
to wish
Not for death
But to never have existed.

Color beneath skin:
Like azure canals cutting beige desert, like twilight over a soccer
    field, like beer bottle caps, like soft-edged sea glass
She told me

Wrapped in a woolen blanket at three in the morning
That she hated herself, because it was all
her fault
Because no one ever told her
She was anything but a disappointment

And I recalled what it felt like
To never be able to separate
From the person who repulsed me the most.

Pressure lingering on my mouth:
Like swollen skin, like being half-awake, like a typewritten letter,
    like soft fog hanging over redbrick buildings
I told her
With my forehead against hers, with my
fingernails in her arm
I wish you saw yourself the way I see you
Like someone
Unlike anyone I've seen before
Like the strongest person I've ever met
Like someone who keeps going
No matter how many times she is told to stop.

Sabrina Ortega-Riek

Small Things

You know how you feel when you reach the last page
of the last chapter
of your favorite book?
Suddenly you're drained and empty and can't remember
what you used to do with your time.
It takes weeks to wash the taste of an ending from your mouth.
And that strange horrible hollowness hides under your skin
    and bobs,
grinning,
to the surface,
when you let your mind wander.

I used to think there was a tea kettle in my chest
and I could feel it whistle,
steam shooting out and piping through my capillaries
until it curled like a dog around my heart.
But only sometimes.
When I sat in the blue-green night while the house slept,
or when dust motes floated, as unconcerned and serene as the
    galaxies above us,
or when I saw places so vivid in my mind's eye I firmly believed
    they existed,
they had to.

Mariah Kreutter

If you wanted.

You have ears
like reservoirs, but
lips that are always
fractured dry.
And your throat
becomes a drainage pipe
for all the words you leave
under your tongue,
but you should really
stopper those ears
and wet your lips
with all these things
tucked in your chest.
We can see
that you think
of yourself
in all lowercase
letters and chicken scratch
scrawl in a world of
capitalization and
size 12 font,
but you should really be
in bold.
The most important words
are the misfit ones
and I want to hear
yours

because you could
press us
into diamonds
if you wanted.

Bailey Flynn

Mind Puzzles

I was a genius because I knew that inside a TV
lived a village of exponents and marching numbers that
advanced inside the maze of a magnetic field, time and
    time again.
The numbers, originally bundled with variables,
were laid out before us like nails in an old man's workshop.
We were trapped between rain and thunder,
between decapitated TV remotes and bitten supreme pizza slices.
The rain outside fell hard but the equations fell harder.

Our eyes were scuba divers, exploring the depth of the Earth,
and our minds too were underwater.
It was too foggy to remember but too dark to learn
that these numbers meant death.

They were violent, stabbing our brains with their sharp edges,
pulling our limbs apart, one by one, then re-gluing them back
    together
as if I were a jigsaw puzzle, as if they were human
and I, a physics problem, an equation.

Laura Wind

10:36 PM

i gave myself away
like so many forced apologies.
my body was never anything more
than a sorry to you:
something that hurt when it wanted to
and gave you hickeys when i meant it.
i filled your mouth up with antonyms
for blame, kissed them into you,
stacked vocabulary up high where your
wisdom teeth should have been.
your tongue would mull me over
thoughtfully, as if your taste buds
were critics of my morality.
then there would always be
one deep hard swallow when my
sorry got putrid in your mouth
and you couldn't spit it out
the way you had made me.

Kae Washington

Unfinished

Those fingertips are bruised

Are they?
Yes, they're mine.
And that person, who I suppose is me,
Hit them against her glass bubble
For the three hundred and twenty-sixth time
This afternoon.

Saskia Levy-Sheon

Quiet, Quiet

The birds died the day you left.
They had their reasons, as you no doubt
had yours.
Because the sky broke.
Because it was mourning.
You tapped an apology from the tip of
your cigarette,
Turned, and walked away.
The ashes settled on the ground at my feet.

Snow-quiet, quiet,
The body of a cuckoo
Drops from the sky.
Upon impact with the ghost,
A final note, a softest—
Bones singing.
I hear it from my bedroom window

sing it back.

See? Do you see?
Cars screech. Disease. Lost
Pets scatter the gutters. Some life.
Memory's-sakes clutter my head
Because I do not wish to look forward.

See? Do you see? I see.
The light is shaking in some ways

You left it lilting
Quiet, quiet to the ground.
Your apology smoldered at my feet until
"I should have swept it dead, then and
there, before,"
It burnt a hole.
Now falling feathers
Swirl, fill the air.

H. K. Law

I Wasn't Expecting That

Startling twists, wit, and unlikely connections

*If I feel physically as if the top of my head
were taken off, I know that is poetry.*
—Emily Dickinson

Prawn Head

Big brother loves to eat prawns
by the dozen. He'd break their
necks sucking down that fatty
headmeat.
Leaving them nothing but a zombified shell,
compliant as you throw them away.
Their use is through.
In between slurps he slurs together
a sentence. Something about
prawns, sharks, and people.
After dinner I take a walk,
past the hammeredheads and the jumbo shrimp of
the neighborhood. Trying to think of ways
to grow hands and feet.

Michael Xiao

Seventeen Years in Review

My friend,
This is 17 years in review.
I want you to have telescopes for eyes
To look past the cloudiness of the skies
And nod slowly when you finally
See the things that you know were never there.

she put our mind games
and secret languages to bed
tucked them under the covers,
murmured a good night or something like that
pulled a gun from under her pillow
a cigarette from behind her ear.

Bailey's is sweeter over ice
A Bug's Life is funnier with Bailey's
The couch is sweaty when we watch *A Bug's Life* together

The shortest route is 2,303 miles
If I said I missed your belly button 2,303 times
would that open the *Los Angeles Times* on your coffee table
to the article of the boy
who tried to smell the tornado
months before it came

The man with words stuck in honey
With grubby fingers, rubs his round belly.
No one knows he gets his strength from the

Nugget of warmth
Tucked behind his lower lip

Can I kiss you
Somewhere secret, hidden in your right brain
So it doesn't have to be
logical, sequential, or rational

It wasn't your bobbing throat
Your droopy eyes
Or your disgusting earlobes.
I just don't want your mother's boyfriend's sister's leftovers

Flaccid chicken skin on the fridge shelf
cheap wine looks wimpy in a snowman mug
dinner is served

a bike ride is the best medicine, I say
almost buzzes as good as the high after a run
but of course there's always slow dancing in Somalia

You taught me how to whittle sticks on the guitar
My shoes were still wet
I played it back to you on the piano

Feeling fat on a Malaysian jungle cruise
is not something to be missed.
Falling asleep next to our anchored, clammy hands
is

My darling,
That was not 17 years in review.
Get microscopes for ears
Because there's nothing you need to hear
That isn't the deep resounding, confounding, bounding
breath that is inside of you.

Coral Lee

I Saw a Dirty Stuffed Rabbit

flailing in the road and
I'm pretty sure it's not a cardinal sin
to run over children's toys
but I swerved anyway

And for a second I thought this
could possibly be Hell and I'm damned
to keep learning the same lesson
like thou shall not run over rabbit-like playthings

After all, only a cruel god
would relish in our shortcomings
and leave a lonesome bunny
to fend for itself in the streets

Isabella Blakeman

Broke

We are broke
six dollars and two cigarettes to buy
rice milk, shampoo, and those dried cranberries
that wedge between my teeth
and make my waltzing taste buds do the electric slide. Before
  I die . . . I have resolved to lie prostrate
on a prayer rug
re-read Karl Marx and wonder when you, my dear, will drop
  the world on my head. And somewhere
there is an objective correlative
to my life. I don't want
your frilly metaphors
your fingernail-clipping rhyme schemes
Listen, I don't want anything, I don't even want
my own life. I sold it
for six dollars and two cigarettes. We are broke.

Savannah Rae Steamer

A Cold

The sick sleep with a mouth open wide
enough to insert the trunk of a growing tree Roots
spread out thicken and Wrap like ribbons

around brain coils, nerves
crying out little vowels in the shape of sound waves
in the shape of sniffles
Emerging like an operatic solo as the pine Grips

the lungs finally Rooted in something warm
out of the cold the birds radiate
cardinals Explore their new home
fly though pockets of alveoli enclose their eggs in capillaries
bees come out of hiding

buzz in the Echo of a struggling voice which rasps
    exorbitant coughs
pleads to stay home
pleads to be rid of this growth inside him
Pleads to quiet the small chirps and organ displacement
this also is how love works.
When we are given time to think

Rose Richard

Fractions

It's three AM
I feel like a third of a person.
And the worst part of that is
I thought quarter in my head.
As the words whizzed like wire signals
from brain to fingertip,
I felt the lie play out
in the tapping of five keys.
A fifth of a person.
Am I shrinking?
I guess the witch of the west
had a point about the whole melting thing
after all.

Kira Carlee

Soft

It's a gray day.
Won't you sit down with me and have a cup
of something hot?
I'd tell you to hold your tongue if
you didn't have such a good grip on it already.
No, that's not my heart rumbling
in hunger for you
No, that's just the thunder.
Won't you sit with me and tell me tales
of things I'm not?
Never mind, just hush.
Try not to slip off that horsehair couch;
I know it's tempting
to let yourself fall.
But keep your eyes locked
and your tongue on something hot
and watch the sky rage.

It's a soft day.
Won't you sit with me and have a cup
of things I forgot
to say?

Mahalia Sobhani

What Is in a Mouth

i always held the Communion wafer
under my tongue
to let it dissolve.
because my mother said you should never press your teeth
into the Eucharist
since it's the bread-flesh of the savior
and so disrespectful to
chew.

i always held my palm open and out flat
with the slice of silver bridle's bit
across my hand like the arrow on a compass's face.
and the horse would
open its chimney rock teeth
and into its mouth
accept its fate.

Sofia Wesley

Healing Old Wounds

When I was seven, the Walmart eye doctor
    told me I needed glasses.
I wore them for six months before I
couldn't stand
the lack in clarity they caused me.

There's a tree in my front yard I used
to climb
no matter what my neighbors thought.
Now it is covered in spiderwebs.

I've never seen a rabbit in the snow,
but they refuse to hibernate—perhaps
because of their determination
to not miss half of their life.
Maybe humans are like that too
Unless sleeping every night is a
    broken-up form of hibernation.
We sleep one-third of our life away.
Or if you're me, one-half.

I wish gravity didn't pull us together
because maybe then my flowers
would bloom
and I could throw a fishing pole to the stars
    in hopes of catching one
to use as a pillow at night
Maybe then hibernating would be worth it.

Humans spend six days a year looking
in the mirror
But I vow to spend zero because
Mirrors are like glasses, they prevent me from seeing clearly.
I can't define left from right
Or what is real or a lie.

My cat wakes me up at the crack of dawn every morning
I squirt her with water, but she still won't
let me sleep.
Maybe there's something to see
I put my glasses away
And climb the tree outside.

Emily Dehr

The Wedding

A man had just married an automobile
The wedding was lavish and large
The man was a Ford who got easily bored
The automobile's name was Marge.
His arms ran like pipes down his
muscular hood
Out of his mouth rose black-sooted fumes
Her doe eyes were large and savagely bright
As if on her visage were two tiny moons.
He retold the story of the day that they met
With a sudden and loud honking sound
She hid abashedly behind rounded,
large hands
As a bottle o' black whiskey he downed.
"He needs it for energy," she told her
bridesmaids
Who considered the match with remorse
They sat on their trunks, sipped mud coffee and tutted
"You could've at least gotten a Porsche."
The strangest part of the ceremony
Was when the priest had let out a shout
For God as his witness, the Bible was empty
The book was blank, all the words had
fallen out.

Tamar Ziff

The Day After

The day after she killed me,
ran me over, riding
a freight train of bad news,
I was uptown. And uptown Donnie,
the homeless bootlegger, thirsty
with a blade,
threatens my already dead self
and steps toward me, while a woman
gives me her number, I wonder,
What does she want with a zombie?
And my head is a mess, I am
walking with a fear of
never arriving, always moving
farther from home. Noticing not
the sidewalk turn to street,
brake pads scream and pupils dilate.
Headlights in my face. I remember
when we were almost roadkill
on the very same street, and I wish
we had been. I would be dead
like I am dead now, but holding your
hand, which now I am not.

Eli Hiebert

Where Do Babies Come From?

Astral shuttles, streaking, dropping
Baby-bearing bubbles popping
Chem reactions for baby brew
Dreamt-up visions 'tween me and you
Eating seeds, growing, retching
Fishing, baiting, baby catching
Gumball babies for a quarter
Hailing babies, sounding mortar
Infomercials, sold on the phone
Junkyard scraps to build your own
Knitted up with some special string
Lightning-born with a sudden zing
Magic genie to grant your wish
Nine-month oven-baked baby dish
Ostrich eggs cracking, breaking
Play-Doh baby, sculpting, making
Quest-assigned for the baby grail
Resent the app sent in the mail
Sneezing, surprise baby snot
Three-D printed little tot
UFOs drop them from the sky
Volcanic-erupted babies fly
Washed up on sands, left to rest
X-marked buried baby chests
You never know where they'll be!
Zero true from A to Z?

I think my parents lied to me.

Tommy Emick

Love, Life, Death
(and other overwritten themes)
Fresh takes on the familiar

A poet's work is to name the unnameable,
to point at frauds, to take sides, start arguments,
shape the world, and stop it going to sleep.
—Salman Rushdie

Written the Week
Following a Funeral

It should have been linen,
the tablecloth. The plastic kind just
don't lie flat.
Plus they smell like
plastic.

I'm the only one who notices, I think.
Everyone else has eased up from the silence
into figure eights
and circular conversations
and side pools;
telling stories,
balancing paper plates
of mayonnaise and cold
pasta.

I should stand with somebody.

It's a broad lawn, a bed
occupied by a body of relations,
blanketed by a hundred stories,
and every mouth is laughing a little,
hanging slightly at the jaw.

The casket was white as a tooth.

As the evening goes on, the alcohol
will start to smell
from mouths and bodies

and stumbling hands will collect ties
and hats,
and we'll all stuff into cars and go to
tell louder stories
over peanuts and cashews
or club wraps and cocktails.
Some of us will talk,
some of us will stare.
We will loosen collars
and laugh widely,
and some will go home to sleep,
or watch TV, or make love,
and wake up to coffee and alarm clocks,
and some of us will sleep in.

But for now,
we are constructed;
a little posture, a little normality
encasing the dead conversation,
pressing on my ears,
smelling of plastic.

Ziggy Unzicker

One Summer

Hey, it's me.

I just wondered if you

(remembered jumping in puddles
in white socks and pressed cotton,
because it was the closest we
would come to touching the sky,
because we could feel it slipping
through our fingers,
and we knew the end before the
beginning.

remembered grass-stained backs
and bemused sheep,
because fields are the home of lovers,
because the ground was fertile,
with a kiss that grew into something more
between the daisies and bracken,
but the skies were never in our
favor.

remembered silent lullabies
and microwave popcorn,
because I was always hungry in
the mornings,
because I was always woken by the light
and you only knew the dark.
because fields grow barren in the winter.)

got my messages. I know how temperamental technology can be.

Shona Louisa Jackson

oil free

At twelve, my mother told me
that going to sleep with makeup still on
would take two weeks off your life.
I know she meant
that I would wrinkle prematurely
and look like my grandmother in my senior pictures
but I still don't wash my face
before I get into bed.
By my estimation, I've got about three days left

Ariel Rudy

Our Finest Cenotaphs

In the future, our lives are pantomimes.
Toward the end sequence
at the funeral of our world,
an old man stands and weeps over the ashes
of syllables, letters, adverbs.
Trying to connect, to remember,
he sends aimless Morse letters to anyone,
our communications of lost existence

The saddest existence I've ever known—
I mean, a ditto of Dostoevsky's Underground Man—
is my great-grandfather's.
In all our family scrapbooks and cutouts,
any observer can almost touch
the shriveling ashes riddling across his face
with no ripple of being alive.
Or others might view being alive as being dead.

Yesterday, I visited him in the hospital.
Fluid jellies and heart detectors uncomfortably
surround him, or what's left of him.
Sitting close by alongside
"Feel better" and inflatable bears
holding lollipop balloons,
I concentrate on the timely counting from the monitor,
the Z-shaped lines that seem to trace
the heart's own writing on its tombstone.

Just now, I learned from the doctors that
his voice was temporarily cut off by
the shock from the heart resuscitation.
Apparently, the larynx, that powerful engine
to fuel our words and language,
was aimlessly flapping around,
barely hanging on to its hinge
before it surrendered,
as we all do.

What I remember now,
two years after the cremation,
is the handwritten note he gave me
in the hospital.
While staring straight at me,
he handed me a white note card
that said, "No words is my cenotaph."
Maybe our future engravings some day.

Keerthi Gondy

The Trooper

1. Raindrops hit the old glass, making
watery cobwebs,
Drowning red and orange traffic lights
in winter.
I wish it would snow.
And hold my breath, struggling to cry
silently.
I turn away from Mom and watch the buzzing Exxon sign.
Swollen in the rain.

2. The hospital light scratches my retinas,
Like an emery board on fingernails clipped too short.
My nose has that piercing pinch that comes before sobbing,
But I sneeze instead,
And Mom steps away from the hospital bed.
"Charlotte, talk to him."

No words. Not about this.
I take my dad's balmy hand, and it tenses meekly.
I watch the nurse.
She watches the catheters,
The tributaries that dip and coil before
tunneling under.
He squeezes my hand. A tiny firm hug.

3. Like a shattered Christmas ornament
Or being as tall as the kitchen table,
You can only cement something into memory
When you know it is gone for good.

Charlotte Zaininger

birthday noodles

Toss the egg in, stir stir stir, crackle
It will pop, yes, it will sizzle.

If we have a birthday tradition, it's
these noodles, plain and simple, just

eggs and wheat and a bit of soy sauce
but cheers to you, we have no wine

but fifteen noodles, all in line, all long.

There's more than fifteen, actually.
Don't make me count them because

noodles always break with bites, and that
will be even worse than counting your

hair single-strandedly, one at a time.
I can count the eggs, though. Toss the egg in

one at a time, one drops, and then there's
two. And if I'm feeling important today

I can count your fingers and count your toes.
If I'm feeling smart, I can count the days

you've been alive, and I can (five-four-
seven-nine) even round to the nearest second.
If I'm feeling dumb, I'll count the socks in
our closet without a fellow pair, and if today,

I just so happen to feel happy, I can count the
days we've been apart and remember how when

you first came from the hospital, you were so
small I thought you were a doll.

Christina Qiu

Trout

On the way to my grandfather's funeral,
We hit only green lights.
Pop-pop's hands felt like a pair of dead fish
flopping over his black suit.
I knelt over the casket to pray
that one prayer our CCD teacher, Mrs. Cazinski,
    had made us recite.
The one with the chin mole
and the annoying daughter
and the heaving breasts.
We stopped to eat on the way home and
my sister ordered fish and chips
and the basket was full of hands
so I did not eat my soup.
On the way home my mother got her second DUI.
A police radio made static while
it began to gently sprinkle
and I counted teardrops rolling down the face
of the basset hound I drew with my pinky finger on the window.

Dan Maddox

Name Tag

Today when you came home you were
too tired to notice you were still wearing your name tag on your
   T-shirt from work. When Dad teased you about it, you smiled
   and replied:
"I remembered who I was today."
and I was so jealous of the way your tongue could unclip those
   words like that name tag at the end of a long day
Like they were nothing
One month
and four days later
I wonder
If you unclipped those words like a name tag because they too
were meant for someone else to read

Andy

When She Stood in the Moon

For some reason, nobody ever mentions Rudy Weidoeft
when they talk about music, or the 1930s, or dry ale. Not even
   liver disease
is real these days. My uncle died seven months ago
from Pepsi, but not really. They just told that story
to his long-divorced wife so that she
could order
an epitaph. The man at the department store
told her that beige accentuated her cirrus-cloud hair
and she bought the dress. For closure, for forgiveness, to look
lovely when she stood in the moon. "Listen to the song again,"
   I say to her
and remove wax wrap packaging
from the record player. Turning over an opaque disc,
I can almost fathom people still listen to jazz. She is
pretending I am still a senseless child while she sits
as a fragile paper doll in the recliner she never bought.
But the music isn't clear anymore, and I wonder
if Rudy Weidoeft ever married. Maybe he did; maybe
she left him before the alcohol even started.
My uncle's bouquet is cherry red and blue, like if I placed it
   to my lips
some tie-dye mark would stain my tongue for good. The woman
who is not quite his wife is smiling for the longest time before
the morgue insists she carry his purple necktie. We sing
   "Amazing Grace" and
bless the stars that never looked over him

Katie Bridgeman

Just Beyond the E-Z Duz It RV Park

Just beyond the E-Z Duz It RV Park and the statue
   commemorating the man who may or may not have been but
   definitely was not Billy the Kid

The gravel has angry marks from
cowboy boots.
Those or little footprints,
because the kids have no need for shoes
when they chase the seventeen dogs
across the field that goes for miles.
Footprints from feet all scraped from thistles
and scraps of leftover wood from building the cat-house
(It really should be picked up).
And the place really should be quiet,
but it can't be
because there's children and seventeen dogs
and screams from the children when they step on a burr
or a dog chomps at their pant leg.

Sophie Lidji

Lester's Will

In the dream, there is an endlessly tall chamber
full of staircases that don't connect.
My father looks up, not a child at all. It is very familiar.
I slip letters and other jewels into my breast pocket
that doesn't exist.
The house is vague like morning, infinitely
secret, and full of dust.

My grandfather is showing those signs
that I love so well. Death rattle like a whisper in his
throat, that faraway look in his eye getting closer.
He pulls his soul back from us, he tucks his body in.
I see that beautiful death haze sinking over him.

Today: snow that fell in the light, the patches
spread out like magic in the yard, the trees rearing back,
laughing, leafless. I ran across the road and clicked
my heels. I am already home, but it felt like the right thing to do.
Bathed in even more light,
the wide, white-rimmed window stretching out in all directions.
The afternoon vast like an ocean; no, vast like a still lake,
quiet and perfect. The bones in my chest spreading
like wings to let my heart out.

Madeleine Chill

Academic Thoughts

I think the whole world exists on a number line
all between one and negative one.
That's as far as cosine will exist.
That's as far as the periodic table goes, too, with the first group's
    charge of +1 and the seventeenth's charge of –1,
except for the noble gases,
which I suppose then must be outside
the realm of provable fact.
Perhaps they are magic.
Hannah says, "What is magic
but a highly advanced science?"
And once in chemistry she said,
"I think God must be a wave."
No one with as many thoughts as that
could exist between one and negative one.
And there are more like her.
They must bleed over into twos and fives and threes and eights,
into colors and noble gases,
into undefined.
Outside the realm of provable fact.
Out where God is.
Where the waves are.

Erika Cook

Nine months and all the seconds

If I ever have a baby
I'll paint his room the color of napkins.
I will find the paint
that carries the tones of mistakes,
of spilling water on the kitchen counter
and cleaning it with thousands of those
paper squares.
I will find the paint
that bounces off the light of bake sales
and using napkins rather than plates
for their simplicity.
I will dip a big brush in a bucket
that holds the memories I have of riding in the car
every morning to school
and eating a small breakfast
that my mom kindly put in that white and soft paper.
I will find this color
and I'll surround my baby with it.
I know my husband will think I'm crazy
when we go to paint stores and I ask for napkin
and they bring me white or beige
and I turn all of them down.
He'll think I'm crazy,
but I don't expect he'll understand,
I don't expect he'll understand my Christmas dinners
and how my cousin and I passed notes
around the family table on those napkins
so we could still talk while my grandparents

gave their Christmas speech.
I don't think he'll understand the summer I worked at
an orphanage and how when I realized there
wasn't toilet paper for my kids to go to the bathroom
I stole napkins from several restaurants
to bring to them every morning.
I don't think he'll understand.
And when my baby grows up
and asks me to redecorate his room
I won't refuse.
I will simply paint over the napkin layers
and I'll make sure he knows all that lies
just a peel away.

Sofia Avila

Where Dandelions Roar

Virginia, stop sinking—
take those rocks from your pockets
and step away from the river.
Let's catch a ride, you and I,
to the place where dandelions roar;
where the alley-cat boys
use their cherry-red lighters
to ignite the stars,
inspired by fireflies
brighter than the sun.

What's your rush, Virginia?
Heaven may be nice
but it may not be there at all
and death is on its way
but Virginia, I'm here now,
and I'll give you some deliverance
à la I-75,
no Sunday dress required.

Think about it, Virginia:
you could drown in your sorrows or
take a dip in the honey pot with me
but either way, Virginia,
promise me

you'll keep trying to swim.

Breanna Bowers

Confession

I like to squint my eyes in the mirror and study the face
    my face becomes.
I like to squint my eyes in the mirror and look for the face
    of a poet,
Or of someone who always matches her socks.
I like to squint my eyes in the mirror and strain to see
    someone for whom the world comes easily,
Because I will never be a person for whom the world
    comes easily.
I know that.
I still wish it would.

I'm not very good at thank-yous, but I'm excellent at sorrys.
I say it's okay to be humble,
But some will tell me to never ask forgiveness,
To take what I can and get out quick,
But they're wrong,
I'm sorry.

Sometimes I dream of taking up smoking and moving to Paris
    and wearing black.
I dream of smoking cigarettes and being caught in the photos
    of tourists who say,
"Look at that Parisian,
Look at her smoking,
She looks like a movie."

I like sitting in churches and watching people pray,
Bathing in stained-glass light.
I wonder if they feel their God inside them,
Loving with their hearts and breathing with their lungs.
I fold my hands and kneel.
I don't think I feel a God inside me.
I feel uncertainty, and blood, and bones.

I think about being in love one day,
Of knowing hands that know my hands
And eyes that know my eyes
And lips that know my lips.
I think about the love that's lost every day
And wonder if it gets recycled,
If it has to be crushed, broken, and melted to nothing
Before it can be made new.
I think about love while I'm looking in the mirror,
But then I get lonely,
So I think about socks.

Abbey Childs

Surrounded by Smoke

I am fifteen
my cat is almost four
and the books I can't live without
are still overdue
at the library
how come everything that tastes good
makes you fat
what if tomorrow
always comes too soon
and the smoke outside my window
won't go away

I have to learn to keep my mouth shut
when they don't actually want to know
what I have to say
my head is throbbing
suppose I left behind
something more than the posters on my wall
maybe even something as big
as a legacy?
my headache isn't ceasing
I can't see clearly
and the smoke outside my window
won't go away

Nobody ever stops to speak
for those who have no voice
I should have tried out for the volleyball team again

they made me captain my first year
why do I have to
be the one
everyone expects to succeed
I have no answers for their questions
will I become the person
I want to be
and the smoke outside my window
won't go away

Whit Jester

wise one

you know so much! they say to me as i rattle
off the bus times—the product of meiosis—
the date of some battle.
you're so smart, love
says my sister whom i adore
(she thinks i know
everything and more).
but there are lots of things
that i would like to learn:
for example, i do not know
how not to fall for someone at "hello,"
or how to keep loving them
or how to let go.

Anna Justine Leader

Poets' Notes

Ayah Alghanem: "Clementines" (77) was inspired by Gary Soto's "Oranges." I never wanted to publish it! I'm glad I did, though.

Andy: "Name Tag" (132) started off as a journal entry concerning my day in a very literal fashion, but I really believe poetry can be prompted by anything, even the most mundane tasks. There is always something to write about.

Sofia Avila: I wrote "Nine months and all the seconds" (137) after realizing that napkins are one of those things that are often around but go unnoticed.

Natalie Baddour: "Fighting the Waves" (16) is a poem for anyone who has ever felt overwhelmed and helpless when trying to overcome life's obstacles. Just take a step back and breathe.

Isabella Blakeman: I have this weird tendency to dig for meaning and backstory in all of those small, wonderfully unimportant moments and objects. "I Saw a Dirty Stuffed Rabbit" (110) was inspired by one of those seemingly commonplace things.

Breanna Bowers: "Where Dandelions Roar" (139) is about suicide. Stick around, because things might get better.

Katie Bridgeman: When I was young, my mom used to tell me that my uncle was not well because he drank too many soft drinks. I still don't drink them to this day, and I wrote "When She Stood in the Moon" (133) as a type of confession to fabricate my memories of and apprehensions about relatives' deaths.

Emma Burn: "to sophia" (70) is addressed to a long-distance friend whom I used to be very close to but have since fallen out of contact with, and describes the last time we saw each other. I think it all happened the way it says, but you can't always be too sure.

Kira Carlee: I wrote "Fractions" (113) because sometimes it's only possible to be honest with yourself at 3 AM, when everything else is dead, asleep, or silent.

Morgan Chesley: I wrote "food and wine" (91)—enjoy.

Abbey Childs: For as long as I can remember, I've struggled with questions of identity. "Confession" (140) is a snapshot of who I was at the time I wrote it.

Madeleine Chill: "Lester's Will" (135) was written after a very vivid and complex dream. It has since gone through countless revisions and rewrites, but this original version will always feel important to me.

Daniel Coelho: Honestly, what inspired me to write "And She Sang as the Chicken Crisped Up" (14) was the scents of my grandmother. Everything sang in her kitchen.

Lauren Combs: I was inspired by my life, as well as various streams of self-consciousness, when I wrote the poem "thoughts?" (13). Visually, it sums up the content of my imagination.

Erika Cook: When I wrote "Academic Thoughts" (136), I was a junior in high school, noticing some similarities between things I was learning in chemistry and trigonometry.

Jessica Covil: When I wrote "O, Father Time" (41), I had been reading a lot of Langston Hughes's poetry and was moving into a new, experimental stage in my writing, in terms of both form and content. Now that I am a third-year at the University of Chicago, I find that the theme of this poem—being a slave to time—is more relevant than ever.

Moria Crowley: In "Genevieve Carnell" (44), I wanted to capture the way I wrote with my friends. It wasn't work or toil—it was banter, pure fun.

Isabel DeBré: "First Law of Motion" (68) is about a time when, sitting in physics class, I found myself daydreaming about a summer kiss. It all seemed connected somehow (not sure my teacher would agree).

Emily Dehr: Writing is in my blood. With that tree right out my window and my glasses collecting dust on the shelf, I had no choice but to write "Healing Old Wounds" (116) about them.

Tommy Emick: I wrote "Where Do Babies Come From?" (120). Instead of the Academy, I'd like to thank my teachers Brian McBride and Angela Beeley. Thanks so much.

Sofia Engelman: I wrote "Smelling Crayolas" (66) in response to the death of a classmate during my freshman year of high school.

Indigo Erlenborn: "Bluebells" (9) is about how sometimes I would rather only remember the good pieces and let the rest fall away. Sometimes I have no choice.

Ilana Feldman: A friend of mine wrote a piece in which he questioned his very existence. "To a friend, in answer to his existential crisis" (48) is my response.

Bailey Flynn: "If you wanted." (97) was written with the intention of reminding readers of their right to speak up. In a world of strong opinions and debate, allowing oneself to fade into omission can appear the safest option, but having the bravery to share thoughts instead of stifling them is worthwhile.

Emma Foley: As I walked along a road I'd always driven down, I was able to take the time to pick up on a lot of interesting contrasts between the urban street and the wide field it sat next to. These inspired the poem "Dandelions" (20).

aiden gamble: I wanted to write and "bread for my soul" (65) is the story that ended up coming out.

Christina M. Gaudino: I wrote "Powder Blue with Roses" (30) so I'd remember that strange feeling standing in church after they took the girl outside. I just think we all say too many things without meaning them.

Keerthi Gondy: I wrote "Our Finest Cenotaphs" (126) at the time of my grandfather's death. It was a very raw and vulnerable time for me.

Isabel Gwara: I was inspired to write "Walk-out" (78) by a concert I went to with a friend of mine. As musicians, we both felt that, despite having to leave at intermission, the music stayed with us. It affected our perception of the world and ourselves.

Eden Hartley: I wrote "Prometheus" (74) for my older sister, Tessa. The night described in this poem is one of my dearest memories from childhood, and I hoped to create something both my sister and I could always remember it by.

Eli Hiebert: My only justification for seeing the end of a monthlong relationship as the end of the world is, well, I was sixteen when I wrote "The Day After" (119).

Miriam Himelstein: I wrote "Year of the Dragon" (12) in honor of a close friend who suffered a terrible loss.

Garrett Hinck: I wrote "I Would Like To" (19) as an expression of my desire to share an experience with a person I cared for.

Rachel Hsu: "Not Enough" (35) was meant to describe a persistent feeling of solitude and unhappiness with myself, despite the knowledge that I was fortunate to have people who love me. Another person's love for you is a blessing, but it never makes up for the lack of love you have for yourself.

Shona Louisa Jackson: One summer I found myself on this crazy, twisting path to growing up. Writing "One Summer" (124) was my way of smoothing over the rough patches.

Whit Jester: I wrote "Surrounded by Smoke" (142) a few years ago when I was in high school. Multiple out-of-control wildfires had filled our valley with so much smoke that you had to wear a mask just to go outside.

Darius Kay: "Like Your Cat" (28) was inspired by John and Joan Cusack, or rather, my personal dream version of John and Joan Cusack.

Mariah Kreutter: In "Small Things" (96), I was trying to capture an emotion I'd never really seen described before but felt was very common.

H. K. Law: I was inspired to write "Quiet, Quiet" (102) by small things, white things, stillness, and silence—the gentle settling of the dust, and the pieces left behind when someone close to you leaves.

Anna Justine Leader: My sister is two years younger than me, and we've had a tradition for a long time of going for long walks together after school and on the weekends. "wise one" (144) is about how I would tell her about things I was learning at school but never felt like I had any real advice to share with her, as I was figuring it all out myself.

Coral Lee: Every year on my birthday, I write a poem "summarizing" and reflecting on the year. "Seventeen Years in Review" (107) is one of these.

Saskia Levy-Sheon: "Unfinished" (101) describes the feeling of alienation that comes from unsuccessful efforts to connect with those around you.

Katie Grey Lewellen: At the time I wrote "It's My Job" (59), I felt that I wanted to write for a living—my parents disagreed with this! I also didn't do too well keeping up, and I felt like self-sabotage was a common theme for me!

Sophie Lidji: I wrote "Just Beyond the E-Z Duz It RV Park" (134) after spending time at my grandparents' house in rural Texas. It's such a different environment from what I'm used to and I wanted to try to capture it.

Sam Little: I wrote "Dear Me, From Me" (52) as a slam poem and didn't really intend to publish it, but my English teacher, Mr. Mongi, convinced me. S/O to my mommy and my dog Reggie!

Hannah Livernois: I wrote "The Sistine Closet" (45) in the midst of an internal war between my religion and my sexuality. Writing to someone I knew would've understood me made me feel less alone in my struggle.

Dan Maddox: "Trout" (131) is a poem about the passing of my grandfather, and how funerals are only tidy for the one in the casket.

Catherine Malcynsky: "my grandmother's kitchen" (26) was inspired by my late grandmother.

Olivia Manno: "Heirloom" (27) was basically a meditation on learning to accept something that initially seemed like a burden to me.

Miranda McClellan: In writing "Welcome Back, Darling" (23), I tried to imagine what it would be like to end a relationship with someone who had wronged me but whom I didn't necessarily harbor hatred toward.

Chelsea McCoyle: I'm sure I'll never see anyone who embodies a Greek myth more thoroughly than the way the subject of "I'll massage your tense shoulders" (22) proved to be Icarus reincarnate.

Ariel Miller: I wrote "Clothesline" (8) about other people's lives during a year when two friends and I challenged ourselves to write a poem every day.

Sabrina Ortega-Riek: "Furrow" (93) is part of a collection of poetry exploring physical and mental illness that I wrote after my grandfather died of lung cancer. It is a poem of affection for those who believe they do not deserve affection and an attempt to create logic within powerlessness.

Samantha Park: "Sincerely, Perspective" (61) is about the experience of self-actualization, the feeling of clarity and self-awareness that once seemed so hopelessly lost. This awareness is such an important part of one's self-esteem and sense of self, and it's something that I was experiencing at the time.

Anna Piper: "Souls Are Not Scientific" (29) is about how love should transcend the physical world and not be reduced to a simple scientific explanation. Love comes from a deep, unexplained place inside us, and it makes us who we are.

Claire Podges: I wrote "Don't Fall in Love" (87).

Christina Qiu: "birthday noodles" (129) was part of a larger collection of ten poems I wrote for my younger sister's fifteenth birthday, which included revelations, reflections, an acrostic poem, and a list of AP United States History thesis statements. This poem, I believe, was the most rhythmic of the collection.

Rose Richard: I was inspired to write "A Cold" (112) after waking up one morning too sick to leave my bed. I remember thinking that the sickness was such an invasion of my person, but also a completely natural occurrence, so I used elements of nature to describe being sick.

Kristian Rivera: I'd like for different readers to get different meanings from "blue base" (56), because my favorite part of poetry is its ambiguity; for this reason, I won't assign a translation to it, but I will say that the piece came from a desire to connect with and relate to other people on an emotional level.

Tia Roberson: "Grams and Tonic" (79) is just about my favorite quirks of my favorite person! My grandma is always cracking me up.

Ariel Rudy: I wrote "oil free" (125) to encourage ending compulsory femininity. Teach your daughters that they are worth more than their faces.

Angela Sabo: My inspiration for "Another Poem About You and the Sink in Your Downstairs Bathroom" (50) was a sink that would drain too slowly at all the wrong times.

Kunal A. Sangani: I wrote "Anonymous, Framed" (64) after visiting Port Jefferson in Long Island and walking along the picturesque docks and bank there. Lingering behind as a friend sat at the dock's edge, I thought of how much the sight looked like a photograph, and what qualities of the town—its quaintness, the breeze—made it feel separate from our daily reel of experiences.

Mandy Seiner: The title of my poem "Write What You Know" (24) is taken from a Mark Twain quote, and the poem is a response to that quote.

Sophia Shelton: "orange hospital bracelet" (38) was inspired by the idea of dealing with tragedy through colors as a distraction or coping mechanism.

Charles C. Siler: I wrote "She" (10) when I was feeling angsty about a girl I knew in high school.

Mahalia Sobhani: "Soft" (114) was inspired by rainy days, the tension of unrequited love, and a conversation with my eleventh grade English teacher. He told us these days are called "soft days" in Ireland, and those who love them are prone to observation and fated to experience a lot of sadness in their lives.

Alana Solin: "serena" (39) and "The Second Coming" (60) were inspired by my sister and by my love of New York, which began before I was born.

Savannah Rae Steamer: My own longing for identity and belonging in a world that I felt did not provide opportunities to people my own age is what inspired "Broke" (111).

Claudia Taylor: I wrote "Pomegranate" (84) for my freshman English class in response to a prompt instructing us to write a poem simply about food. Pomegranates are one of my favorite foods, so I decided to write about how I feel when eating them.

Meredith Thomas: "a preposterous poetical proverb for practical people" (34) was one of a collection of poems I wrote for an English assignment. It was inspired by my own social ineptitude.

Eda Tse: I was inspired to write "chinese politics (over dim sum)" (42) during a dim sum lunch (Cantonese food served in baskets) that I attended with my mother and her friends. There was an undercurrent of tension and pride in the conversation, so I turned that feeling into a poem.

Ziggy Unzicker: The only funeral I've been to was nothing like the one in "Written the Week Following a Funeral" (122), but I've been to many other events like it. "My Hands Are Empty" (88) was inspired by a lovely dance with a great friend of mine. We never did get the waltz down.

Andrea Wade: I wrote "knees on neon (a hymn)" (92) when I was fifteen, and nothing I said was backed in any life experience.

Christal E. Walker: When I was a senior in high school, so many options were before me, and I was feeling flustered, nervous, and excited. "After All This Time" (36) captures those feelings: apprehension and the sense of time both speeding up and slowing down.

Kae Washington: I wrote "10:36 PM" (100) because I felt like my emotions needed to be heard. It just so happened that they were heard at 10:36 PM.

Beatrice Waterhouse: Being queer and Jewish informs a large part of my identity, especially since those aspects of myself are ever-changing. Both "Jazz Girl" (85) and "Reading at the Lake" (72) speak to some part of me, as best they can.

Claire Weaver-Zeman: My experiences swimming and sailing at the beach in the summertime inspired me to write "More Summer" (11).

Sofia Wesley: In my lifetime, I've been the bully and the victim. I originally wrote "What Is in a Mouth" (115) and "A Letter to the Past, Present, and Future Selves" (32) to raise the confidence levels of victims and bullies and show them they are not alone.

Laura Wind: "Mind Puzzles" (99) is in essence a reminiscence of my childhood at its finest. My main inspiration was the memory of sitting down next to my oldest brother and observing as he practiced for his quantum physics degree.

Michael Xiao: "Prawn Head" (106) is an allegory for society, with themes of government, power, and individuality.

Julie Yue: I wrote "inverted biography" (17) as a part of NaPoWriMo (National Poetry Writing Month) my senior year of high school.

Charlotte Zaininger: "The Trooper" (128) is a poem for anyone going through loss.

Kalina Zhong: "impatient" (81) was written after I'd gotten back from a rather prestigious college fair—my dad and I thought we'd just take a shortcut, but then we found ourselves stuck for over twenty minutes waiting for a train to pass. I immediately was reminded of the college search—and how no matter how many shortcuts I wanted to take, there was no getting around this very large (and very frustrating) obstacle.

Tamar Ziff: I composed "The Wedding" (118) during a summer writing course in Jesus College, Cambridge.

Callie Zimmerman: As an artist, I find it is most effective for me to use drawing as a metaphor for my relationships with people. In "Charcoal Boat" (31), I wanted to use the fragility of charcoal to reflect on how people often leave.

Michal Zweig: I lived by a lake when I wrote "With Every Atom of My Being" (57), and I liked watching people interact by it. During the summer, the colors of nature and people were all really beautiful; thus, this poem was born.

About the Editors

Stephanie H. Meyer, senior editor of *Teen Ink* magazine for twenty-six years, is also the creator and editor of the widely recognized Teen Ink book series. She holds master's degrees in education and social work and has dedicated her life to the welfare of youth. She and her husband, John, have two children and three grandchildren.

John Meyer, MBA, is publisher of *Teen Ink* magazine. He works to keep the business side of the magazine functioning and has spearheaded the evolution of Teen Ink's website.

Adam Halwitz, Teen Ink's book development editor, joined the magazine's staff in 2007. As an intern and later an assistant editor, he's read and evaluated thousands of teens' poetry submissions. He graduated from Marlboro College in 2014 with a degree in philosophy and writing.

Cindy W. Spertner, editor, has been working for *Teen Ink* magazine for seven years. With a background in education and an MA in writing and publishing from Emerson College, she is thrilled to be immersed in great writing and helping to make a positive difference in the lives of teens.

Index of Titles and First Lines
First lines are shown in italic

Permissions

"Clothesline." Reprinted by permission of Ariel Miller. © 2011 Ariel Miller.

"Bluebells." Reprinted by permission of Indigo Erlenborn. © 2012 Indigo Erlenborn.

"She." Reprinted by permission of Charles C. Siler. © 2012 Charles C. Siler.

"More Summer." Reprinted by permission of Claire Weaver-Zeman. © 2012 Claire Weaver-Zeman.

"Year of the Dragon." Reprinted by permission of Miriam Himelstein. © 2013 Miriam Himelstein.

"thoughts?" Reprinted by permission of Lauren Combs. © 2013 Lauren Combs.

"And She Sang as the Chicken Crisped Up." Reprinted by permission of Daniel Coelho. © 2014 Daniel Coelho.

"Fighting the Waves." Reprinted by permission of Natalie Baddour. © 2012 Natalie Baddour.

"inverted biography." Reprinted by permission of Julie Yue. © 2011 Julie Yue.